The Lindisfarne Gospels

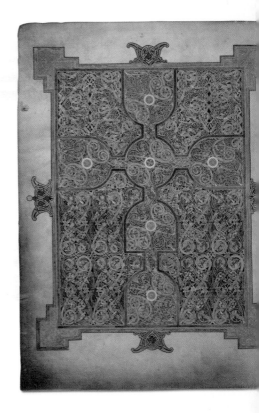

OPPOSITE AND LEFT Cross-carpet page and opening (incipit) page of St Matthew's Gospel.

THE LINDISFARNE GOSPELS were made around 710–20 on Holy Island, off the north-eastern coast of England in the Anglo-Saxon kingdom of Northumbria. This remarkable volume is now one of the nation's leading artistic treasures and an icon of faith, preserved in the British Library.

The book is a copy of the four Gospels, along with St Jerome's prefaces to his Latin Vulgate translation, and is adorned with illumination of breathtaking artistry. The Gospels' opening words explode across the page in an exuberant riot of ornament, enlivening the elegant calligraphy of the text – literally the Word made word – and become sacred images in their own right. They are introduced by cross-carpet pages, a device of Egyptian Coptic origin recalling prayer mats, with the sign of the cross embedded in an intricate warp and weft of decoration composed of birds and beasts. The Gospel writers are depicted as exotic, mystical icons, redolent of the arts of the eastern

Mediterranean. A subtle concoction of artistic ingredients is employed: curvaceous, swirling Celtic spiralwork; plaited interlace, often formed of living creatures, of the sort made fashionable by the Germanic peoples who settled in the late Roman Empire; Roman capitals of the kind found in inscriptions along Hadrian's Wall, combining with Greek Byzantine letter forms and the angular shapes of Germanic runes. This heady mix combines to celebrate the new identity of the islands of Britain and Ireland, and their role in the wider world, in a living act of prayer.

In the mid-tenth century the Latin text was glossed in Old English, added between the lines, by Aldred at Chester-le-Street, where the Lindisfarne community had relocated. It is the oldest surviving translation of the Gospels into English.

A visit to the place of the Lindisfarne Gospels' birth makes it easy to appreciate how such beauty and inspiration came about. Holy Island (Lindisfarne) is a tidal island, which is cut off from the mainland twice each day, and where the rhythm of life is subject to the tides and seasons. It is a place to think and to be. On a fine day the murmur of the breeze, the lap of the waves and the cry of the curlew are the only disturbances. On a stormy, wind-lashed night it is another matter completely. What must life have been like for the monk who made the Gospels? Monks and nuns had to rise eight times every day and night to attend Divine Office. They had to prove humility by undertaking manual labour as well as prayer and study. If, as seems likely, the Lindisfarne Gospels were made by Bishop Eadfrith of Lindisfarne (698–721), he would also have had a heavy administrative load, overseeing the pastoral care and local government of much of northern England and southern Scotland.

Amazingly, this book, one of the most complex works of art ever made, was the work of just one person – an *opus dei* (work for God), undertaken as a hermit in emulation of Christ in the wilderness and St Cuthbert (died 687), the great bishop-saint of Lindisfarne. When not out providing humanitarian aid and preaching hope, Cuthbert lived an austere life on the barren nearby island of Inner Farne.

The artist-scribe was a gifted calligrapher and illuminator, a fine textual scholar and a technical innovator, who seems to have invented the lead pencil and the equivalent of the lightbox to enable him to devise such an elaborate new layout. He was also a skilled chemist, capable of emulating the entire palette available to the Mediterranean world, with its extensive trade links, from a handful of local substances: green (copper); red/orange (toasted lead); an incredible range of blues and purples from plant extracts (woad and folium); yellow (arsenic); white (chalk or shell); black (carbon). He is unlikely to have used magnification to focus in upon the complex details of his work – but we can do so today, with the aid of digital photography, opening up the inner life of the Lindisfarne Gospels as never before.

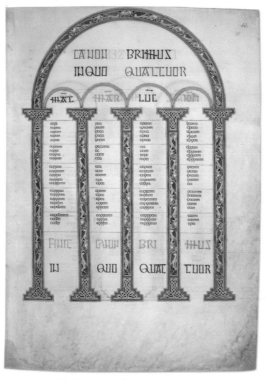

A canon table (Canon VI).

St Matthew portrait.

OPPOSITE Detail showing Eadfrith's final unfinished work on the opening St Jerome carpet page. Did illness or death intervene?

RIGHT Detail resembling a textile from Coptic Egypt. Carpet pages were partly inspired by Eastern prayer mats (also sometimes used in Europe).

BELOW Corner piece from the St Jerome carpet page with two dog heads, resembling a Celtic metalwork mount.

peric

mech   ne ddg.

IUMENO ELOCEBERIS

INECURREUS ADPRINCI

DICITINQUIB: CANONUM

ET DISFUNCTA CONTENUES

DOEM Q: FUITINCANONE

EXCACULO SNOTTAS INUECTO

UUIN QUEM QUI AEREBAS

IUMENUM EIUS DEN

EUUANGELISTAE QUI AIPSE

XIIUSCRIBTAONE SIGNAUIT

UUENIES ATQ: EUIANIA

CETERORUM TRANTAB:

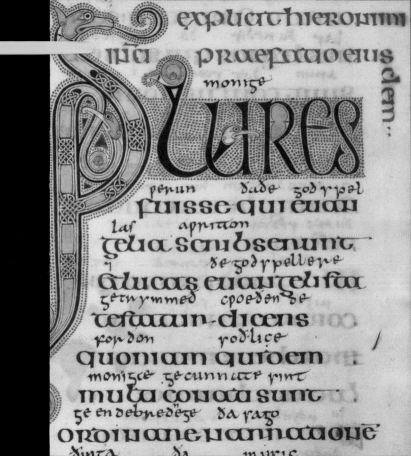

explicit hieronimi

praefatio eius

dem··

monige

PLURES

ꝼerun · ꝺaꝺe · ꝫoꝺ ꞃ ꝼel
fuisse qui euan

las · apꞃiꞇon
gelia scribserunt
⁊ ꝺe ꝫoꝺ ꞃ pellere
& lucas euangelista

ꝫeꞇꞃymmeꝺ · cpoeꝺen ꝺe
testatur dicens

ꝼoꞃ ꝺon · ꞃoꝺlice
quoniam quidem

monige · ꝫe cunnaꞇꞇ ꞃinꞇ
multa conati sunt

ꝫe en ꝺeꝺneꝺeꝫe · ꝺa ꞃaꝫo
ordinare narratione

INCIBIT BRAEFA

Title (above and below) and
initial (opposite) commencing
the letter from Eusebius to
Bishop Carpianus explaining
how the canon tables work.

TIO EUSEBII:

CANON

INQUO

HMĀT   HMĀR

cccx	ccci
cccxiii	cccviiii
cccxviii	cccvi

BRHHUS
QUATTUOR

LUC

cocain
cocain
cocai

ɣcain
cbcci
cloain

Detail from Canon Table I, showing passages that
appear in all four Gospels. From left to right are
Matthew, Mark, Luke and John. The roman numerals
in the columns are repeated in the margins next to the
relevant Gospel passages throughout the book.

ABOVE Initials and display lettering for the prefaces to St Matthew's Gospel. The 'Ma' on the left combines beast heads symbolising Mark's lion, Luke's calf and John's eagle in harmony with Matthew's Gospel.

OPPOSITE Opening of the chapter summaries for St Matthew's Gospel, marked by marginal roman numerals in red. Aldred glossed this opening heavily in Old English.

St Matthew
portrait, emphasising
the relationship
between the Gospels
and Hebrew scripture.
The latter may be
symbolised by the
green book held by
the figure behind the
curtain, perhaps
Christ, who inspires
Matthew to write
his gospel.

Matthew wears
Mediterranean-style
classical sandals, their
form not very well
understood by the
northern European
artist. His feet rest
on a footstool, which
floats like a magic
carpet.

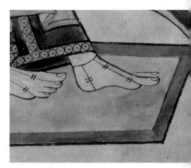

RIGHT Preliminary drawings for the St Matthew portrait, which was painted on the other side of the leaf (the colours can be seen showing through). The faint drawing shows that a larger corner piece for the frame was intended (note the circle beneath the number 24).

OPPOSITE St Matthew's symbol, the man, representing Christ's humanity, is here shown as the trumpeting angel of the Last Judgement, thereby linking Christ's Nativity with His Second Coming.

imagohomi

Detail of Matthew's Gospel being written. Eadfrith did not write and decorate an already bound book, however. Double pages were laid out separately, working out how many words to each line

and page. Decoration was planned by laying out designs on the back of pages to be painted. To enable this, Eadfrith seems to have invented the lead pencil and backlighting (forerunner of the lightbox). He would have worked on a transparent glass or horn writing board with either a large window or many candles behind it, and a weaker light source behind him. This meant that he could both see the designs when painting on the other side and turn the leaf over to consult his detailed drawings. Turn to the next page and you will see the final result.

RIGHT The arms of the Latin cross embedded in the ornament of the Matthew carpet page take the form of chalices like those used for the wine in the Eucharist (Mass). The white circles may have been intended to be gilded, recalling metalwork rivets holding together processional crosses. The jewelled cross was a symbol of resurrection.

OPPOSITE Carpet page of St Matthew's Gospel (detail).

bóc

incipit euangelii

genelogia mathei

PREVIOUS PAGES Decorated incipit page carrying the opening words of St Matthew's Gospel. The decoration blends Celtic spiral work with Germanic animal interlace, including a knot of four birds, perhaps symbolising the four Gospels.

ABOVE Eadfrith blended Greek, Roman and angular Germanic Runic-style lettering to emphasise the collaboration between their church traditions. Note the Greek character for 'f' in the second occurrence of the word *filii* (shown here is *filii david filii Abraham*).

OPPOSITE Chi-rho page. The sacred name of Christ was sometimes written as 'xpi', an abbreviation of the word *Christi* in Greek letters. Here it introduces the Nativity and explodes across the page, celebrating the Word. The line of script outlined with red dots is unfinished and the artist may have intended to gild it.

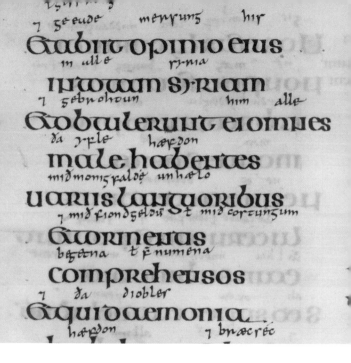

7 ʒeeude menʒunʒ hiʃ

ꝺꜷbιτ opιnιo eιus
in allẻ ʃꝺnιꝼ

ιnττꝛꝛꝛin syꞃιꝛꝛ
7 ʒeꝺnohꝺun him allẻ

ꝺꝺbτꝺleꞃunτ eιomnes
ꝺꝺ ꞃ̇ple hꝷꝺꝺon

mꝺle hꝷbenτes
miꝺmoniʒʒꝺloẻ unhꝷlo

uꝺꞃιιs lꝷnʒuoꞃιbus
7 miꝺ ꝼιonꝺʒeloẻ τ̃ miꝺ coꞃτunʒum

ꝺτoꞃmenτꝺs
beʒ̇ꝺnꝺ τ̃ en̄umenꝺ

compꞃehensos
7 ꝺꝺ ꝺιobleʃ

ꝺꝺquιꝺꝺemonιꝺ
hꝷꝺꝺon 7 bꞃꝷꝺꞃéꞃ

<table>
<tr><td>34</td><td>The colourful column of initial 'b's (opposite)
introduces the Beatitudes in St Matthew's Gospel.
Their interpretation obviously challenged Aldred, who
glossed them extensively in his distinctive, minuscule</td></tr>
</table>

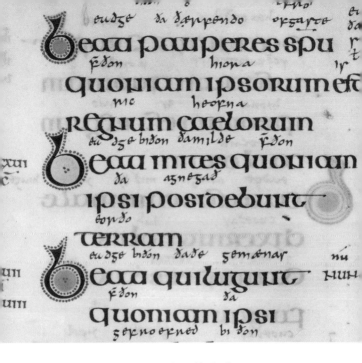

hand, which contrasts with Eadfrith's larger script, which is known as half-uncial. The numbers in the central margin correspond to those in the canon tables.

incipit
MARcus

de gospel
etan
in pulpit

lone goder 7 pet her

gebsca di Ceptri Inbap
yunu   7   Ingod cund
usmace filius acq: Inditui

ABOVE Initial commencing the prefaces to St Mark's Gospel, ornamented with dog-like beasts, recalling his symbol, the lion.

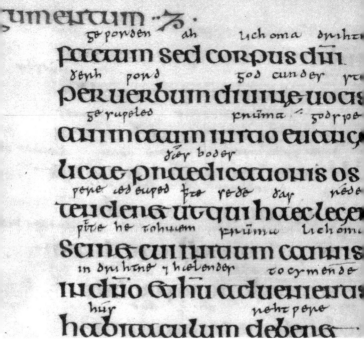

ᵹe poꞃðen   ah   lichoma   ðꞃihtꝺ

factum sed corpus diu

ꝺeꞹh   ꝑonꝺ   ᵹoꝺ cunꝺeꞃ   ꞃꝺ

per uerbum diuine uocis

ᵹe ꞃuꝼeleꝩ   knuma ꞉· ᵹoꝺ ꝑe

carnm catm iurao euanci

ꝺeꞹ boꝺeꞹ

licae praedicationis os

ꝑeꝑe ioꝺ euꝼeꝺ ꝼꞃo ꞃeꝺe   ꝺaꞹ   neꝺa

teudens ut qui haec legen

ꝑꞇe he ꞇohuꞇam   knuma   lichoma

Scinc cui iurdum caruus

in ꝺꞃihꞇne ⁊ hꞝlenꝺeꞹ   ꞇoeꞹmenꝺe

iucio echu aduenieras

huꞹ   nehꞇ ꝑeꝑe

habitaculum debens

OPPOSITE St Mark with his symbol the lion, signifying kingship and resurrection. Note the delicate pen-work of the lion's fur.

imago leonis

ABOVE Initial opening the chapter summaries for St Mark's Gospel, with two dog-like lions and St John's eagles.

OPPOSITE AND OVERLEAF The St Mark carpet page. On the back drawing (opposite) the compass and grid marks used to establish the layout can be seen in the central roundel. The interlace was drawn freehand. On the result (overleaf), note how the roundel has the perspective of a raised metalwork boss, of the sort that sometimes covered relics on jewelled and stone crosses of the period.

40

OPPOSITE Incipit page bearing the opening words of
St Mark's Gospel. This is a cross-section of the initials
INI. The background is occupied by interlaced beasts
formed of red dots. Some decorated pages carry several
thousand dots, each one made as a prayer.

ABOVE St Luke and his symbol, the calf or bull,
representing the sacrifice of Christ at the Crucifixion.
Note the winged calf's finely drawn hair and feathers.
Saints Matthew and Luke are shown bearded and
ageing because they symbolise Christ's humanity
and are mortal.

OPPOSITE Initial 'Q' from the incipit page beginning St Luke's Gospel. The centre of the Q is filled with designs stemming from Celtic prehistoric metalwork. Eadfrith began filling the triangles with gold leaf but did not finish. At the head of the page he has written the name of St Luke and his symbol (*vitulus*, meaning 'calf' or 'bull') and the Chrismon symbol denoting Christ, using expensive powdered gold ink, one of the earliest uses of gold in manuscripts from Britain.

RIGHT Four swirling spirals from the centre of the St Luke carpet page, recalling the four evangelists.

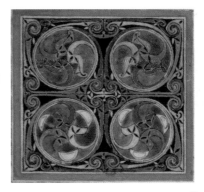

LEFT Panel of interlaced birds from the Luke incipit page, recalling a woven Byzantine silk of the sort imported into Britain.

OPPOSITE A solemn procession of birds marches across the lower border of the Luke incipit page, oblivious to the cat, symbolising temptation, that waits to pounce. He has already swallowed a number of birds, his full stomach forming the right-hand border. To the right of the cat can be seen the back-drawing for an initial on the following page.

QUIDE ☩

moriʒo   cunnendo

IULICO

poeᵹon   ftehiu   ʒe

UNCORDINA

ʒa

ATIONEM

TERTIO COMMENDANS

mid hracing honda

EXTENSIONE MANUUM

tahte þ him þte nodes

SIGNIFICAT EI QUOD CRUCIS

deaða vereoybeand mid dromz

MORTE FORET MARTYRIO

seisgfertnad

CORONANDUS

quae lectio cum in natale

san petri legitur

a loco in coatur

quo ait

Ait simoni

petro ihs simon

iohannis

explicit secundum
Iohannem

Scī iohannis
apostoli &
euangelista
post epiphania
dnĩca prima
post ephifania dnĩca
secunda
Inuelanda
In dedicatione scē mariae
Dnĩca ii xl gisima paschae

PREVIOUS PAGES Initials from the prefaces to St John's Gospel. Aldred did not translate all the prefaces into English because they were not all still used (these relate to readings for Church feast days in Naples, where the model for the text probably came from). Here we can regain something of the original appearance of the elegant layout before Aldred added his gloss.

OPPOSITE Portrait of St John with his symbol the eagle, who soars to the throne of God for inspiration. The enthroned figure of John, youthful and immortal, also represents Christ in Majesty. His piercing green eyes challenge the viewer. The image sits like a framed icon on the page, the thick pink background recalling images painted in wax from the eastern Mediterranean.

OVERLEAF St John's carpet page, perhaps the most complex of them all. Its rich interlace, composed of birds, invokes Creation interwoven in harmony and united with the Cross. One bird stands out for its plain pink and blue striped wings, perhaps emphasising that the harmonious whole is made up of individual creatures.

Decorated incipit page commencing
St John's Gospel. An exotic blend of motifs from cultures
stretching from the deserts of Syria to the watery
wilderness of the Atlantic. Animals that originated in
Syrian hunting scenes inhabit the same world as the
seabirds of the Farne Islands, whilst ancient Greek key
patterns float amidst waves of interlace.

Detail of the display lettering from the
St John incipit page. At top right is the only human-
headed letter in the book, perhaps St Matthew's
symbol, the man. On the line below is the head of
St John's eagle, and in the centre of a letter 'd' on the
fourth line is the dove of the Holy Spirit. Just above
this Aldred's gloss reads 'God feder' (God the Father).

Et quomodo tu dicis
ȝedæfnað ꝥte se ahæfen t
oportet exaltari
sune monnes
filium hominis
huelc is ðes sune monnes
Qui est iste filius hominis
cuæð forðon se hælend get t
Dixit ergo ihs adhuc
lytel leht
modicum lumen
miðh is
in uobis est
ȝeongas ða hwile leht
ambulate dum lucem

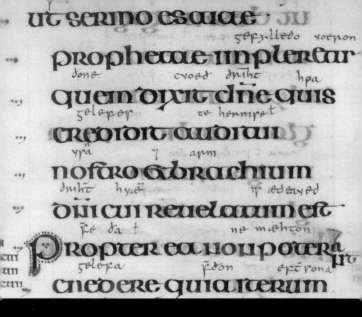

ut sermo esaiae
prophetae inpleretur
quem dixit dne quis
credidit auditui
nostro ɛ brachium
dni cui reuelatum est
Propter ea non potera
credere quia iterum

Aldred used red ink to gloss St John's Gospel as it
enjoyed particular prominence in Early Christian
thought. John was considered a visionary, and his
Gospel was used to minister to the sick and the dying.

It was sometimes used as a talisman, and a little copy
of John's Gospel was interred with St Cuthbert inside
his coffin, like the Egyptian Book of the Dead.

59

qui scribendi sunt
boec *& rodlice*

libnos · amen :~

aræd *ir t.* *þ boc*

EXPLICIT LIBER

aept

SECUNDUM

io *han · nem*

IOHANNEM :

ðed in fulde & ðean fulde god ðir god   *spll* *sie ðe p*
sytruie
ðortlycðu
æ secula con

☩ Trinus & unus ðm evangelium hoc ante
scipt *lauuit* *oer myde cuipt*

☩ Matheus exone xpi scripsit

oer myde *patet* *ueruut*

☩ Marcus exone petri reuips

oer myde *puuier* *uruut*

☩ Lucas deone pauli ap genips
indigil niri tiseragu ridda noezecede t

☩ IOh. in prochemio deinde enuetuauit
pona mit ala

OPPOSITE Aldred added a colophon in the blank part of the book's final column, after the final 'explicit' marking the end of John's Gospel. He starts by naming the four evangelists, and those from whom they received the Word: Matthew from Christ, Mark from St Peter, Luke from St Paul and John from the Holy Spirit.

Eadfrið biscop lindisfearnensis ecclesiæ

he ðis boc awrat æt fruma gode 7 s̄c̄e

cuðberhte 7 allum ðæm halgum ða ðe

in eolonde sint. 7 Eðilvald lindisfearneolon

his hita gidryde 7 gibelde fra he wel cuðe

7 billfrið se oncre he gismioðade ða

gihrino ðað utan on sint 7 hit gi

hrinade mið golde 7 mið gimmum æc

mið sulfre of gylded fa conleag feh

7 aldred þæn indignus 7 miserrimus

mið godes fultume 7 s̄c̄i cuðberhtes

hit of glosade on englisc 7 hine gihamad

mið ðæm ðrim dælum. Matheus dæl

gode 7 s̄c̄e cuðberhte. Marcus dæl

ðæm biscope. 7 lucas dæl ðæm hionode

7 æhtova reolfnes mið to mlude

7 s̄c̄i ioh dæl þ hine reolfne 7 feover ora

hæbbe ondfong ðenh godes milse 7 s̄c̄i cuðberti. þte he

reel 7 ribb oneonda fond geong 7 sidhrigo

virdom 7 snytro ðenh s̄c̄i cuðberhtes earn

Eadfrið. Oeðilvald. Billfrið. Aldred.

hoc evange dō 7 cuðberhto constryxerunt

OPPOSITE Aldred goes on to name those who were thought in his time to have made the book originally – Bishop Eadfrith of Lindisfarne (698–721), the artist-scribe; his successor as bishop, Æthilwald (721–40), the binder; Billfrith, the anchorite, who adorned the book with gold, silver and gems; and Aldred himself, who completed the work by translating it into English – the oldest surviving translation of the Gospels in the English language. He thereby draws a comparison between the original evangelists and the four latter-day evangelists, with himself equating to the visionary St John.

RIGHT Aldred glosses his own colophon, and here gives some autobiographical detail. It translates as 'Aldred son of Alfred is my name, son of a good woman, of distinguished fame'.

The British Library would like to thank the following for their help in producing *Treasures in Focus: The Lindisfarne Gospels*: Michelle P. Brown, Bobby Birchall, Charlotte Lochhead and Patricia Burgess.

All the images are taken from British Library, Cotton MS Nero D. iv. p. 1, f. 211r; pp. 2–3, ff. 26v–27r; p. 8, f. 11r; p. 9, f. 25v; pp. 10–11, f. 2v; p. 12, f. 3r; pp. 14–15, f. 5v; pp. 16–17, f. 8r; pp. 18–19, f. 11r; p. 20, f. 18v; p. 21, f. 19r; pp. 22–3, f. 25v; p. 24, f. 25r; p. 25, f. 25v; pp. 26–7, ff. 25v–26r; pp. 28–9, f. 26v; pp. 30–1, f. 27r; p. 32, f. 27r; p. 33, f. 29r; pp. 34–5, f. 34r; pp. 36–7, f. 90r; p. 39, f. 93v; p. 40, f. 91r; p. 41, f. 94r; p. 42, f. 94v; p. 43, f. 95r; p. 44 (top), f. 137r; p. 44 (bottom), f. 133r; p. 45, f. 137v; p. 46, f. 139r; p. 47, f. 138v; pp. 48–9, f.139r; pp. 50–1, f. 208r; p. 52, f. 209v; p. 54, f. 210v; p. 55, f. 211r; p. 56, f. 211r; pp. 58–9, f. 241r; p. 60, f. 259r; pp. 62–3, f. 259r

First published 2006 by
The British Library
96 Euston Road
London
NW1 2DB

British Library cataloguing in Publication Data
A catalogue record for this book is available from
The British Library

ISBN 0 7123 4951 0

Designed and typeset in Berkeley by Bobby & Co, London
Colour reproductions by Dot Gradations Ltd, UK
Printed in Italy by Printer Trento S.r.l.